More Dreams Alive

Kathleen Lorden
Boylan Catholic High School, Rockford, IL

More Dreams Alive: Prayers by Teenagers

Edited by

Carl Koch

Saint Mary's Press
Christian Brothers Publications
Winona, Minnesota

Genuine recycled paper with 10% post-consumer waste.
Printed with soy-based ink.

Karen Esker, cover artist, Saint Pius X Catholic High School, Atlanta, GA

The publishing team included Carl Koch, development editor; Rebecca
Fairbank, copy editor; Barbara Bartelson, production editor and type-
setter; Stephan Nagel, art director; pre-press, printing, and binding by
the graphics division of Saint Mary's Press.

Printed in the United States of America

Printing: 9 8 7 6 5 4

Year: 2003 02 01 00 99 98

ISBN 0-88489-321-9

Contents

Joe Mackowiak
Marian Catholic High School, Chicago Heights, IL

Preface

In May 1991, Saint Mary's Press published *Dreams Alive: Prayers by Teenagers.* Because of the enthusiastic response to that book, we decided to do this sequel: *More Dreams Alive.* Consequently, in October 1993, I sent out a letter to religious education chairpersons in all Catholic and selected Christian high schools and parish religious education programs throughout the United States, inviting them to collect prayers and reflections of their students. The letter said: "The topics the students choose to write about can be virtually anything that deals with concerns or themes of high interest to young people. The selections may be funny or serious, focused on themselves as individuals or on other people, perhaps even reactions to national or world affairs. Most important, we are looking for writing that reflects honesty, authenticity, and an awareness of the real world of young people." I believe you will find that the prayers we selected have all these qualities.

To ensure spontaneity, I asked that the students not be told the prayers were being written for possible publication. When teachers had selected prayers for submission, the writers were given the opportunity to attach their full name, initials, or first name, or to remain anonymous. All the prayers were identified by the school or parish from which they came.

Prayers and reflections poured in from all over the country: Massachusetts to California, Washington to Florida. By May 1994, I had hundreds of pages of writing to work with. The sheer number, the quality, and the diversity dazzled me.

I began reading, sorting, and selecting. After an initial sorting, I asked six students to help with the final selection: Erin Hansen and Paul Zobitz from Saint Mary's College of Minnesota, and Liza Bambenek, Mary Costello, Tim Vessel, and Joe Wilzbacher from Cotter High School, Winona, Minnesota. Kim Vogel, campus minister at Cotter High School, graciously coordinated my work with the Cotter students. The team of students studied the prayers and helped select the ones that appear in this book. Their contribution was indispensable and is greatly appreciated.

Using the Prayers

If our experience with *Dreams Alive* is any indication, teenagers, religious educators, youth ministers, and retreat staff will find the prayers useful in a variety of settings and situations: to start a class, to give focus to a prayer session, and so on. Many of the prayers can also trigger discussion about topics important to teenagers.

Before starting a prayer, you may wish to recall God's presence for your group. Such a reminder calms people and prepares them to attend to the prayer being read. To assist you, three different calls inviting God's presence are listed at the beginning of each part of the book (see pages 11, 35, 49, and 73).

Many of the prayers have final lines that close them nicely. However, after reading a prayer, you may wish to invite those praying with you to share insights or petitions related to the prayer. Or you may want to give people a moment to pray silently.

This book of prayers could also be a helpful gift to parents of teenagers. The prayers can remind adults that despite appearances sometimes to the contrary, teenagers have a unique and lively perspective on faith, the world, and themselves. The prayers may open avenues of much-needed teen-parent communication.

A Final Word of Thanks

Great thanks are due to all the students who allowed their prayers and reflections to be submitted for consideration. The only unpleasant aspect of editing this book was having to eliminate so many wonderful prayers. They just could not all go into the book. So, I thank all of you for your contributions and understanding.

The art used on the cover and the illustrations inside the book were also contributed by students. The gift of their work is gratefully acknowledged.

Thanks also go to all the religious educators throughout the United States who sent in the thousands of prayers received. Your cooperation made the book possible.

I hope all who pray these prayers find consolation, inspiration, and great hope.

Carl Koch
Editor

Dan Powers
Marian Catholic High School, Chicago Heights, IL

1
Personal Matters

Recalling God's Presence

- Let us remember that God is with us now.
- God, be with us now as we pray.
- Gracious God, we stand in your presence to pray.

Prayers

Dear Jesus,
Please help me to have the courage to follow my dreams.
Help me with the determination to carry them out.
Give me the patience to deal with negativity,
the fortitude to accept defeat or failure.
Give me the strength to overcome my barriers.
Strengthen the hope that motivates me.
Give me the desire that makes my will strong.
I know you have given me what it takes to be a success;
please help me to use it to my best potential.
Help me to give what it takes
to be my own success.
Amen.

Dan Francis
Marmion Academy, Aurora, IL

How can it be?
All these problems piled right in front of me.
No one to turn to, no place to go,
all these problems trapped inside of me.
I feel as if I'll explode.
Dear God, what shall I do
to become more patient, self-confident,
    and compassionate
just like you?
They say every one lives life for a purpose.
Now I'm confused.
Some people are victims of abuse and neglect;
shall we say their purpose for life was to be used?
Is there any way possible for me to find out,
before my time on earth is gone,
if I've taken the wrong route.
You see I'm trying to figure out now if so far I've
    done good
in trying to follow your footsteps the best way
    I possibly could.
Is there a way to figure this problem out,
so I won't have so much doubt?

Evelyn Hill
Saint Martin de Porres Academy, Chicago, IL

Dear Saint Francis,
I never knew your story, but when I found out how you
discovered happiness by being a servant to those who
once served you, I developed a unique respect for you.
You seemed so fearless toward life, so prepared. You were
sure of what you wanted, even in a time of such intense
corruption. Nobody seemed to see the faith diminishing
until you gradually cleared their vision. I admire you for
your brave soul and your undying love of God. To be like
you would be an amazing accomplishment.

To be honest, I don't tell anybody how I feel about God and my faith. Jesus is my best friend, but how do I tell that to my best friend here on earth? If I even try, they call me nuts. It's true, I hide it. My mother thinks I'm wrong in my ways. She thinks I'm lying when I tell her that I pray nearly every day and then some, but I do.

My dream is to find completeness in so little, like you did. I am sincere when I say people do not understand me. I don't even understand myself. I want so desperately to be good like you, but I am constantly messing up. How do I say I can't do it on my own?

My mind is blocked at times and God disappears from my thoughts. When I think of all the simple temptations I give in to, I get upset with myself. I wish I could feel as content in humbling myself and raising the lowly as you did.

I am selfish, it is true, but not so selfish as to believe my actions and, no doubt, my words are always correct. I have no gift of eloquent speech, nor a gracefully powerful voice. My sins outnumber the miles to the sun. Yet I know what I feel is growing stronger day by day. You began your life so unaware, but in one moment you discovered what you wanted from your life—to give to the world.

My gift from God is God's presence in my everyday decisions. I possess the gift of what we like to call common sense. Out of my many bad decisions, I have learned small but countless lessons. I see the truth in the life of Jesus, and it grows with each inspiring story, like your own. I have not done this on my own; I learned to guide myself in the right direction when it finally came to me: "There is a God!"

I believe God strengthens my heart to listen to my call. I wish I knew what made you so strong. That is my dream: to understand.

Maria Mast
Notre Dame Academy, Covington, KY

Dear God,
Thank you for my body and mind, which help me perform my tasks in life.

I ask that you sharpen my senses so that I can feel the pain of others, the pain I have became numb to because of today's society.

I ask for the power to resist pride that is undeserving. Let me accept responsibility and independence fully.

Please give me the wisdom to accept help from others when I need it.

Thank you, God, for everything you have given me. Amen.

Ben Tate
Saint Pius X Catholic High School, Atlanta, GA

God,
I can recall a time that my mind
closed itself off to you,
I shut out your words,
and narrowed my mind.
I have long since learned,
that closed-mindedness is the real sin.
I was miserable in my solitary world
without you.
Forgive me the times I've done this
to you and myself.
But . . .
How you energize and empower me,
when I open myself to you.
How you forgive my foolishness,
and bring me back.
Thank you. . . .
Amen.

Ivan D. Dominguez
Salpointe Catholic High School, Tucson, AZ

God,
Why did you make growing up so hard?
Everyone always says these are the best years of my life.
If they really are, why do I go through so much misery
    and strife?

Sometimes I feel like I'm on top of the world without
    any fears,
but in all reality I feel pressured to fit in with my peers.

I'll never know why I try so hard to fit in,
but deep down inside I know that you are my true friend.

You'll love me and lead me and forgive all my sins.

Maxine F. Bynum
Saint Maria Goretti High School, Philadelphia, PA

Dear God,
How can I tell what is right for me? Decisions are tough
for me. Life is confusing. Many little things become inten-
sified when it comes to making decisions.

I'm often afraid that I will make the wrong decision,
and it will come back to haunt me sometime in the
future. In today's world every decision needs to be made
carefully. One wrong choice could change the whole
direction of my life.

I pray to you, God, to help me in making these decisions and to guide me through life. The path I take will be
determined by these decisions, but hopefully with your
guidance I will stay close to you.

Joe Kita
Saint Mary's of the Assumption, Scottsville, NY

Jesus, I thank you
for your gifts
of love and forgiveness.
Your love has sustained me in painful times,
and your comforting presence has helped me
when I have felt abandoned.
Please, continue to be with me
as I grow,
and guide me on my path.
Help me to remember
that each day is a gift
in which I am given the opportunity
to serve you.
Amen.

Holly Doyle
Mount Mercy Academy, Buffalo, NY

Dear God,
You have made all things. You sculpted the planets and
created human life. I don't have to look long at a sunset
or a rosebush to know that you are the greatest and most
talented artist in the universe. Still, God, sometimes I
don't feel beautiful. I know that you have created me so I
must be special, but it's hard to feel that way sometimes.
My hair seems ugly, or my clothes don't feel right, or even
worse, I feel ugly inside.

Please, God, help me to feel beautiful inside and out
because I *am!* Help me to remember that I am poetry,
sculpture, song, and painting. Help me remember that I
am a masterpiece created by the greatest artist ever.

Angela Meyer
Bethlehem High School, Bardstown, KY

God, I put my faith into your hands.
You are my sole support in these
unsure times.

Where can I turn when it seems
no one has the answers to my questions?
God, I turn to you.

I am full of youth,
yet I am not immortal.
Who can I call on when the friends
I need the most are too busy?
God, I call on you.

God, I put my faith into your hands,
You are always there,
never too busy.
You have always been
my best friend.
Out of everyone who loves me,
you love me the most.
And you are just a prayer away.
God, this is my prayer.

Asheley Riley
Academy of the Sacred Heart, Bloomfield Hills, MI

As I looked at myself one day in the mirror,
I saw my reflection and started to sneer.
I always looked different, certainly not the same,
the looks that I had, gave me no fame.
Then suddenly I looked way down in my heart,
and found I had something that set me apart.
As I found this inner beauty that will always
    shine through,
I looked up to God and said, "Thank you."

Corrie DeTella
Queen of Peace High School, Burbank, IL

Oh, dear God, please tell me why
every day I start to cry.
Others talk behind your back making fun of you.
You feel as if you've been betrayed
and nobody loves you.
Every day I'm killing myself
about three times a day.
I can't fight this disease,
I'm trying to find a way.
Life isn't fair.
You can't win.
Nobody's perfect.
I don't understand what is happening.
I'm really scared.
I can't leave this alone.
Can you answer my prayer?
Please, dear God,
don't let me cry.
Help me through this,
so I don't die.

Gina Calderone
Maria High School, Chicago, IL

When the pressure to succeed seems overpowering,
    and that helpless feeling of failure begins to set in,
    help me to realize alternative paths to my goals.
When the future appears too frightening to face
    and independence is an ominous unknown,
    help me to have faith in myself and my ability
    to handle life on a personal level.
When death slides its dark shadow
    over everything believed to be real,
    help me to understand its purpose
    and overcome its impossible pain.

Teresa Davidson
Routt High School, Jacksonville, IL

Dear God,
All of my life I've been told what to do, but choosing you
has been the best decision I've ever made. You've stuck by
me through everything, even when I didn't think you
were around. Sometimes I question you, and I'm sorry.
Saying, "everything happens for a reason" is confusing,
but I think I'm starting to understand. You work in such
secretive ways. Well, maybe they're not secretive, but just
not seen by those not allowing you into their lives. Letting *me* experience so young a deeper sense of *you* reas-
sures my faith and trust. Knowing you are right here with
me makes me feel special.

Allison Vasilj
Marian Catholic High School, Chicago Heights, IL

Dear God,
I feel like a broken-up puzzle, pieces of life scattered to the
wind. I know each piece fits somewhere special, but alone
I cannot make the pieces fit. I remember that your Son's
life puzzle was difficult, but piece by piece it began to fit
so perfectly. Help me by giving me guidance. By the Holy
Spirit, help me to fit my pieces together, for now they are
scattered far apart. My life is complete chaos. I pray, help
me to complete my puzzle by giving me guidance in my
actions, decisions, and duties. I wish to be closer to you.

Ann Taksas
Marian Catholic High School, Chicago Heights, IL

Dear God,
Help me through the times
in which I think you just
don't care, or that you aren't
really there.
Help me through times that are
rough, and even when it isn't
that tough.
And most of all, help me to
realize that your love is
infinite and always, always
definite.

Scott Noone
Boston College High School, Dorchester, MA

Holy Spirit,
Give me *wisdom,* so I can learn from my mistakes and
    help other people.
Give me *counsel,* so I may have someone to lean on
    in times of need.
Give me *reverence,* so I may show how I love you.
Give me *courage,* so I may stand up for what is right,
    so I may achieve my goals without hurting others.
Give me *understanding,* so I may try to understand people
    better and not get angry with them.
Give me *wonder,* so I may respect what the Creator put
    here and love it even more.
Give me *knowledge,* so I may learn about my faith,
    my world, and myself.
Let me use and develop these gifts so I can act more like
    Jesus. I try hard, but I sometimes fail. Once again
    I ask for *courage* to get up and try again. Amen.

Charles Brace
Canevin Catholic High School, Pittsburgh, PA

Dear God,
Only fifteen months left until I graduate.
My teachers, my parents, everyone,
tells me I should be making choices
that will affect my whole life . . .
that these are some of the most important decisions
I will ever make.
And I can't even decide what TV show to watch
or who to take to prom
or if I like chocolate or plain milk better.
There are so many colleges to see,
so many tests to take,
so many decisions to make.
It's overwhelming.
Help me to not grow up too fast . . . to stay carefree
and appreciate youth while I still have it.
Did Jesus always know what he was destined for?
Did his divinity protect him from human fear
    and uncertainty?
Or did he, too, need your support;
did he need your strength to help carry out your will?
Please send me a sign.
Help me to realize what my secret ambitions are. . . .
Help me discover your plan for me.
Guide me toward the person you want me to become,
and give me the courage I need to become that person.

Kathleen Callahan
Rosary High School, Aurora, IL

God, help me understand myself a little bit better. Help
me to cope with the things in life that are important to
me. My life can be stressful if I don't take it one step at a
time, but I know you'll give me the strength to survive.
I know that with your help it will be possible.

YoKatty Hernandez
Saint Mary High School, Jersey City, NJ

Help us, O God!
Bless us, O God, for we are your children.
Let your strength and love flow into us so we can become
closer to you.
Let your Spirit shine upon us so we may see your light.
Let your healing hand come upon those who are suffering
from emotional pain so they can be healed by the
power of your love.
Let your unconditional love provide us with the strength
to survive everyday life.
By your strength, your Spirit, your unconditional love,
and your wisdom, we are able to live our life to its
fullest.

Kryssie Herrera
Corpus Christi Academy, Corpus Christi, TX

How easy it is to be thankful
when things go my way!
How easy it is to be kind and helpful
when not much is asked of me!
How easy it is to love someone
who loves me in return!

How hard it is to be thankful
for the courage to try again when I fail.
How hard it is to be kind
when words and actions hurt me.
How hard it is to love someone
who is unlike me.

God, give me strength.

Nick Rice
Christian Brothers High School, Memphis, TN

God,
When I'm afraid of the future, give me the courage to take what comes, turning adversity into opportunity.

When I'm paralyzed by self-doubt, coax me out of my shell so that I can know my talents and use them in service to you and to others.

When I feel unlucky to be alive and when I'm convinced that no one else shares my problems, remind me of your many blessings that surround me.

And as my eyes are opened to the wonder of your creation and I find peace within myself, know that I thank you and praise you with all my heart and soul.
Amen.

Margaret Walsh
Saint Benedict High School, Chicago, IL

Oh, dear God, how foolish I am.
I spend my precious time trying to please those
    around me.
I get distressed when others disagree with me.
I am disturbed whenever I am misunderstood
    by my peers.
But, God, I am learning to trust in you because
I read in your word that you knew me in my mother's
    womb.
You molded me into a unique human being.
You say that you will never leave me
and that you will always guide me.
So in the future, let me keep all things in perspective.
Let me not be so concerned with pleasing other people,
but help me to seek to please you, living God. Amen.

Chris Haven
Brother Rice High School, Bloomfield Hills, MI

God,
When my last game is played, when the final whistle is blown, when the buzzer goes off, when the cheers finally cease, when Coach calls our final time-out, and when the stands no longer have people filling them, something does not seem right. No more ankle tape, no more warm-ups, no more high-fives, no more trash talking, no more wins, no more losses, my adolescent career is over.

Please guide me through the next stage of my career: adulthood. Amen.

Kris Tungohan
Saint Elizabeth's High School, Oakland, CA

Jesus confides:
"I am the lake,
And you are the fish.
Roam where you like,
And do what you wish.
I give you a home,
A place that is safe.
Please stay close by,
And don't fall for bait.
This place that I give you,
It's a wonderful place.
It's a place of happiness and love,
Not a place of horror and hate.
I shall show you around,
So you do not get lost.
I will show you a way,
A way of no cost.
I shall guide and protect you,
And keep you away from sin.
If you somehow get out,
I will help you back in."

Joann Bute
Columbus High School, Waterloo, IA

Dear God,
I need your help. I have learned through Alateen that I
can turn over my problems to you as I understand you.
I never understood you completely before, and I still
don't. I know that I can trust you to listen openly and
continue to guide me when I am willing to listen. Please
help me to understand my problem and to find a possible
solution. I feel lost, confused, and frustrated. Why does
it seem that my life never stays together for more than a
couple days? I have made wrong choices in the past. Help
me to make this one and future decisions right.

Anonymous
Bishop O'Dowd High School, Oakland, CA

When every day seems like a challenge,
when every day doesn't seem worth living,
I close my eyes and pray
that God will keep me from my despair.

When every day is so difficult to get through,
when every living day drains my strength and will,
I close my eyes and try to remember
that God is with me.

When living becomes too painful,
when life seems too empty,
I remember that God knows
of my pain, fears, and frustration.

When sadness overcomes me,
I close my eyes
and pray . . .
for love.

Elizabeth Ahn
Cornelia Connelly School, Anaheim, CA

Help me, O God,
I have fallen into peril and can't find a way out.
The days and nights have no meaning to me,
for I have been accused of sin.
Help from you, O God, is the only thing
that can save me.
I have become an outcast from my own friends
   and family.
Has my sin been so terrible
as to destroy all relations with those who love me?
Have I stained my name to the point
that people stare at me in disgust?
Why would people who are like me want to destroy me?
I know that I am not of the finest people,
but I try to follow your law and abide by it.
I constantly feel the eyes of those
who would be glad to see me destroyed.
God, you are the only one who sees truth.
You are not blinded by greed, anger, or distrust.
Judge me fairly, my God.
I ask for forgiveness from you.
I pray that others learn to forgive, too.

Santiago Morales
Christchurch School, Christchurch, VA

Dear God,
Sometimes things seem unbearable. I know that you are
always with me, but sometimes it is difficult to believe
and to feel your presence. The Scriptures tell us that you
know when we sit and when we stand. You are always
with us. Your dwelling place is each of our bodies. Help
me to remember that you are with me and in me, and in
each of the people around me. If I know and believe this,
I will never have to face my struggles alone.

Molly Molloy
Billings Central Catholic High School, Billings, MT

Dear God,
I haven't been the perfect child.
Although I try and try,
I make mistakes and lie sometimes
Not even knowing why.
But when I feel I've done the worst,
And all my feelings could just burst,
I know you will forgive me in the end,
Because you are my friend.
Please save me from the evil ways
And help me through my days.
For without your guidance and the love you give me
I would be lost, my God, so forgive me,
Please.

Michelle
Immaculate Conception Church, Greensburg, IN

God,
I often find myself worried about school, deadlines, and all of the things that seem so important in my life. Sometimes I concentrate more on getting good grades than on truly learning something. Sometimes I concentrate more on success and achievement than on what kind of person I am becoming. Sometimes I find myself wishing for another weekend instead of making the best of my life one day at a time, moment by moment.

Help me to understand that I can find real happiness only when I can concentrate on "being" rather than "doing," and on "becoming" rather than "achieving." It is in this that I can truly experience you. Amen.

Rebecca Losinno
Saint Basil Academy, Fox Chase Manor, PA

Dear God,
Help us to be strong when we feel weak.
Help us to love when we feel as if we can't love anymore.
Help us to be humble when we are arrogant.
Help us to find the right path in life,
to know which way to go when we come to a fork
in the road.
We know life is a puzzle; help us to put the pieces
together.
Help us understand that you will give us the strength
to carry out your will in our lives. Amen.

Anonymous
Coast Episcopal High School, Pass Christian, MS

Give me the courage to do right
in the face of wrong.
Instill in my heart
a set of values that prompts me
to think of others
instead of just myself.
Give me the willingness to
stand up for what I believe in—
not following the crowd.
Give me the strength to
look evil in the eye
and withstand it.
Because I know
with you at my side
all things are possible.

Theresa Vonderwell
Saint John High School, Delphos, OH

God,
Make my body strong,
so I can do your will.
Make my mind strong,
so I can think good thoughts.
Make my heart strong,
so I can love everyone.
And make my soul strong,
so I can be open to you and to your Son, Jesus Christ.
Amen.

Marcella Ortega
Saint Catherine Indian School, Santa Fe, NM

God,
You are wonderful and full of wisdom. Right now I am
young and do things without thinking of the conse-
quences and without thinking of how it will affect me
later. But you see the whole picture and know when I am
straying from your ways. Please help me to make the right
choices about my future. Give me the patience to take
one day at a time. Amen.

Crystal Kadrmas
Trinity High School, Dickinson, ND

Sometimes the odds are against me.
Sometimes there seems to be no hope.
But I'm strong in God
who gives me strength to cope.
"Be strong and steadfast
and don't fake it.
Be strong in the Word
and you're gonna make it!"

William K. Dowdy
West Philadelphia Catholic High School, Philadelphia, PA

Lift this heaviness away.
Send pillows of light to cushion my night.
Kiss my soul.
Hug my mind.
Touch my thoughts.
Let calm fall into my night.
May sleep come soon.
Free me from all that shakes me.

Anonymous
Institute of Notre Dame, Baltimore, MD

To All That Is Infinite,
Thank you for the spirit and potential of human beings.
Lead us to see the hidden beauties of life and the many
wonderful paths available to us. Let us learn to see our
lives as blank pages, full of potential. Help us integrate all
that we know into a unified whole. Inspire us to see the
world with wonder and learn to appreciate all that is.
Enlighten us to grow to a deeper understanding of one
another. Amen.

Sarah Jones
Villa Duchesne/Oak Hill School, Saint Louis, MO

Dear God,
Be with me when my parents are pushing me to go so far.
Be with me when school has me stressed out.
Be with me when my team is losing.
Be with me when a family member is this close to death.
Be with me when the troubles of the world
all seem to be on my back.
Through all the times of my life, O God,
please be with me.

Anonymous
Saint Edmond High School, Fort Dodge, IA

What's life really about?
Trees and birds, little boys and girls.
It's something one can't understand.
I have no idea.
I wonder about many things.
Maybe God is really simple,
but everything is so complicated.
Why killings?
Why disasters?
Life is about believing in
something.
A God.
Believing God will answer
all your questions
when you meet
face to face
if you ever do.
And about wondering,
hoping
maybe trying to stop the
impossible
like killings, disasters.
It could happen
if you believe.
Life is so
confusing.

Greta Spitz
Pacelli High School, Stevens Point, WI

Dear God,
My life is like a roller coaster. One second I think it's high and mighty, and the next it is down and low. But I know that all these ups and downs are finally going to come to a stop. I'll get off that roller coaster, and I'll be the best that I can possibly be.

You have given me the gift of freedom of choice. Although I may not make the right choice all the time, I do learn from my mistakes. I really can't put into words how to thank you for all you have done. I just want you to know that whether I'm on the top or the bottom of that roller coaster, you're always with me. I thank you!

Melissa Mifflin
Vincentian High School, Pittsburgh, PA

Dear God,
Help me not to put off till tomorrow,
for tomorrow might not come.
Help me to say "I love you" to all loved ones,
before the day is done.
Help me not to hold grudges,
and help me to forgive others.
Help me to work hard in every way,
and help me reach my goal everyday.
Help me to be the best person I can be,
for my gift to you is the life I lead.
I ask your help, O God.
Amen.

Kristy Pannone
Stella Maris High School, Rockaway Park, NY

Matt Letourneau
Boylan Catholic High School, Rockford, IL

2

Friends and Family

Recalling God's Presence

- God, our friend, you are with us as we pray.
- Holy Friend, you are present among us.
- Be with us, kind God, while we pray.

Prayers

With my hands folded together
after I bless myself tonight,
I raise my head to heaven
and open my heart wide.
I ask Jesus
for strength and courage,
and pray to God
to bless my family and
keep safe all who are near me.
I thank God for every given
breath of this day
and hope that God will grant me
yet another wonderful day.

Courtney Kierst
Saint Mary's Regional High School, South Amboy, NJ

36

Dear God,
Before I say anything more, I'd like to thank you for all that you've ever given to me. I know that without your guidance, I wouldn't have the things I have now.

Please help me to understand better the reasons why my friend died. Since he died, I often think about him and how much I miss him. I still come to tears at times. At least now I realize that I must spend as much time as possible letting those I care for know how I feel about them. Please keep him safe with you in heaven and have mercy on his soul. Let him know I care about him, miss him, and hope to see him again. Thank you.

Jonilyn Ramos
Mercy High School, Middletown, CT

God, I have come to understand the correlation between happiness and wishes. If on my first of three wishes, I wished for personal happiness, with whom would I share my joy? If on my second wish, I wished for the happiness of my family and friends, what of those whom I do not know? If on my third wish, I wished for the happiness of all persons everywhere, what is the need for the first two wishes?

The joy of my family and friends would be my joy, and the happiness of all people would bring happiness and light into my life and the lives of my loved ones. God, although this seems simple in my mind, please help me to apply this to my life, and perhaps someday I can help make this world a place where no wishes for happiness are needed.

Rebecca Elizabeth Miller
Marian High School, Bloomfield Hills, MI

God,
you have blessed me with the precious gift
of friendship.
My friends mean the world to me.
We laugh, cry, fight, and celebrate
together.
We share our secrets, our fears, and our regrets.
We share our joys, our successes,
and our lives.
My love for my friends is great,
and I will always stand by them,
as I know they will stand by me.
True friendships are unique.
When you have given us the ability
to truly trust and love our friends,
we come to a better understanding
of your sacred love for us.

Lisa Podowski
Marian Catholic High School, Chicago Heights, IL

God,
I stumbled across my parents' photo album while I was
looking for my jacket. I saw my father's pictures of when
he was in the Vietnam war. I look a lot like him at twenty
years old. You know, in many ways, I see a lot of my
father in me, and I'm sure he sees much of him in me.
I love my father, and I'm proud of the fact that he is my
dad. I might grow up to be like him, maybe even better.
But, I know that I will never be the man he is.

God, I ask that you continue to guide my father in
raising me up right, and I ask that you continue to watch
over my family and guide us on the right path. Amen.

Joe Boyce
Immaculate Conception High School, Elmhurst, IL

God,
So understanding is mutual, and decisions are for
        the best . . .
So feelings are expressed easily, and decisions can be made
        with others' feelings in mind . . .
So fights are not forever, and we can take the steps to
        resolve conflicts . . .
So everyone has good memories and doesn't
        look back . . .
So the person we care for will always be there for us,
    and that we will be caring for the right person,
    and that God will guide our happiness . . .
For everyone to have someone special to care for
    and to be cared for in return . . .
For these gifts, I pray.

Judaline Swinkels
Notre Dame High School, Belmont, CA

Thank you, God, for special people.
When I needed a friend, and not one was to be found,
they welcomed me with their warm embrace.
When I felt hopelessly lost,
they took my hand and graciously showed me the way.
When I felt like I could no longer continue,
they supported me with strong dedication.
When I didn't understand,
they patiently shared their words of wisdom.
When I needed a prayer,
they gladly spent moments with God for me.
Thank you, God, especially for grandparents,
for they have filled that space in our hearts
that is reserved for the most special people in our lives.

Kelly Casey
Saint Bernard's High School, Saint Paul, MN

Dear God,
I thank you for letting me get up this morning. I ask you
to bless my day and my life as I go on my journey to get
closer to you. I ask you to watch over my family and
friends so that they can live in your love. I'm very grateful
to be alive and to serve you. I close this prayer in your
name. Amen.

Jomari Holder
Bishop Loughlin Memorial High School, Brooklyn, NY

Wanted:
Someone who will talk to me,
Let me listen, let me learn.

Wanted:
Someone who will listen to me,
A kind ear that will not turn.

Wanted:
Someone to say "It's all right,"
Who will be there when the nightmare stops.

Wanted:
Someone to say "I love you,"
Who will help fill the emptiness inside.

Wanted:
Someone whom I can trust,
Someone whom will stay by my side.

Wanted:
A pair of arms willing to give a hug,
A voice to whisper, "The nightmare will end,"
A hand to wipe the tears away.

Wanted:
A friend.

Donna Webb
Our Lady Academy, Bay Saint Louis, MS

Sometimes I feel all alone. There is no one to turn to and, if there is, I wonder if I can trust them? That is when I met you, my friend. You were a person who was a true, ideal friend. A person with a sense of humor when I was depressed; a person I could trust and depend on when everyone else was against me; a person who sacrificed everything just to help me. A friend like you comes around once in a lifetime. However, I wonder if I give to you as much as you have given to me?

Dear God,
Please help me to be a friend to all.
Help me to forgive those who have hurt me,
and help our friendship begin to grow again.
Please help me to remember all the things
that my friend has given to me,
and help me to live up to my part.
Help me to remember the meaning of friendship.
Amen.

Janine Popalis
Cardinal Brennan High School, Ashland, PA

Dear God,
Mrs. Diane Messina was a close friend and colleague of my mother's at the Kingston Elementary School. Before I was born, she began working as an aide for my mom in her special-needs classroom. So I have known Mrs. Messina my entire life. During these years I grew to know and love her as family. Mrs. Messina was the type of person who put the needs of others before her own. As an example, although money was not plentiful in her household, she would not hesitate to buy an ice cream for a number of students in the cafeteria because she felt badly for them. And she was always the first one to bring in a turkey for needy families at Thanksgiving time. She was by far one of the most loving, generous, and caring

persons I have known. Mrs. Messina died suddenly last June. Sadly I attended her funeral on my fifteenth birthday. I now view life differently.

Death. I have a hard time accepting this reality. I understand that everybody passes at some time or another. Yet it does not seem real. Mrs. Messina was here one minute, but gone the next. It is a situation that is almost impossible to comprehend. Although I know that she is living a far better life with you, God, I wish that she was still here with all of her friends and family. But if she were here, due to her condition, she would not be leading the kind of life that she would want to live.

I miss her dearly. When I go over to my mom's school I expect Mrs. Messina to come walking down the ramp holding a stack of papers that she had just run off and saying, "Shev, where is my picture of you?" Still the one memory that stands out most vividly in my mind is the talent show in my sixth grade. I sang "The Wind Beneath My Wings," and all I could see out of the corner of my eye was Mrs. Messina watching me, smiling and crying. Even today I sometimes feel her presence looking down on all of us, and she's still smiling. Please take care of her, God. Amen.

Shivonne St. George
Archbishop Williams High School, Braintree, MA

Dear God,
In a world facing poverty, misfortune, and disease, I think it is essential to thank you for what I do have. Thank you for beautiful nature in which I wake up every day. Thank you for a family that I can always lean on for support. Thank you for my friends who make each day special enough to get up the next. Thank you for guiding me thus far through my life and being there through it all. Most important, thank you for life. Help me to more fully recognize your presence in my life. Amen.

Mike Streit
Marmion Academy, Aurora, IL

Dear God,
Sometimes I feel like I don't belong anywhere and that I really don't have a purpose in this world. I find it difficult to always be honest and true to myself and others. But I thank you for lending me the most understanding and trustworthy friends. They are my way of communicating with you.

I regret not always giving you the time you deserve. Please help me to take time out and give of myself to you, any way possible, whether it be in community service or personal sacrifice.

Amen!

Teresa DeWyse
All Saints Central High School, Bay City, MI

At first, this Christmas seemed to be an ordinary Christmas. All was normal, except that the eldest Turpin was not there; he had died three months ago. I noticed a change in my grandmother's attitude, and at one point at night, she decided to present to her two sons the gifts my grandfather left them: a ring and watch that had been passed down through the family. My father, who by now was teary-eyed, received the ring box. This was odd because the ring was supposed to go to the eldest son, and when my father, the younger, got it, all faces showed surprise. It didn't seem quite right until the moment he opened it. Just as he opened the ring box, the song "Ave Maria" came on the radio, and it never sounded so beautiful. It was the same song that my grandfather requested as his wedding song, fiftieth anniversary song, and his funeral song. Now everyone in the room felt as though the "Ave Maria" on this Christmas night had been planned by my grandfather.

Brian Turpin
John F. Kennedy Catholic High School, Manchester, MO

God,
Why do I always feel this way? One minute I feel I have so many friends and at other times I feel like a lost sheep in a flock. I get lonely sometimes—to be honest, most of the time. I feel like everyone is enjoying their friends except me. I am not going to say I don't have friends, but I feel that I just don't fit in with my friends.

Everyone I've spoken to has said that you meet your true and lifelong friends in college, but I don't want to wait that long. There are too many things that are going on in my life. I pray to you, God, that you widen my circle of friends and help me to have healthier relationships. Amen.

Tiffany Norflin
Cabrini High School, New Orleans, LA

God, thank you for blessing me with a loving, caring, and wonderful family. My family is very important to me even though I don't always let them know that. They offer me emotional support and are always around when I need someone to talk to. I know my problems and worries probably seem small or stupid to my parents, who have much bigger problems, but they never let me know that. They take the time to listen to me and offer advice from their life experiences. Even though I don't always follow their advice, it's nice to know they care enough to share a part of themselves with me. Watch over them, God, and keep them safe in your care.

Bill Taylor
Xavier High School, Middletown, CT

In our darkness, God is the moon, watching over us. The stars are a good symbol of the many people in our life who love us: our parents, grandparents, brothers, sisters, teachers, and friends who are always there to listen, to share some encouraging words, to lend us a smile when we're feeling hurt, or to rejoice with us when we achieve happiness.

God, help me to realize that I am never alone or forgotten. Thank you for surrounding me with so many beautiful people who love me. Give me the courage to thank them. But above all, God, thank you for illuminating the way for me.

Noelle Midlock
Joliet Catholic Academy, Joliet, IL

God,
I am young and don't know or understand what it is like to be a parent, but it must be very hard because so many people are failing at it these days.

I pray for Mom and Dad, God, that you will help them to be good parents, strong in ways you want them to be, so I can look up to them with admiration and feel confident that their instruction is right.

Help me, dear God, to understand my parents. Remind me that when I don't get my way it is because they love me, and not because they want to be mean or deprive me of a good time.

Help me, God, when I become stubborn and refuse to listen. Help me accept the fact that they have wisdom and experience because they were once teenagers, but I have never been a parent.

Put in my heart the respect and consideration they deserve for their years of hard work and sacrifice. They are raising me the best they can. Let me not repay them with grief or shame. Rather, help me to give them obedience, respect, forgiveness, and love. Most of all, God, while I still have my parents here on earth, help me to appreciate them and let them know that I do! Amen.

Lindsey Krebs
Bishop Ryan High School, Minot, ND

God,
Thank you for giving us another day to spend with our friends. Often in our discussions of violence in society, we forget that there are some weapons that do not leave visible wounds, but hurt just as much. Contrary to a popular saying, words can hurt. Today, let us be mindful of what we say to our friends. Sometimes while joking with them we say things that we think are funny, but that hurt or offend. Help us to use our words to express friendship and love instead of sarcasm.

Julie Schweitzer
Visitation Academy, Saint Louis, MO

When my friends search, God,
Help me be part of their journey.
When my friends stumble, God,
Help me catch them.
When my friends hurt, God,
Help me carry them.
When my friends fall, God,
Help me pick them back up.
Help my friends know I'm there for them, God,
And help me know they're there for me.

Jamie Gudmastad
Cotter High School, Winona, MN

Dear God,
Please help me to be a good friend to everyone. Often I
am caught in the middle of two feuding friends, and I feel
forced to close my mind to one and take sides with the
other. I know that I should not do this, but sometimes
after hearing bad things about someone over and over, it's
hard not to believe them. I never really know what to do
in these situations, so please give me the wisdom to do
what is right. Amen.

Cielo de la Paz
Cornelia Connelly School, Anaheim, CA

A friendship is like a sunrise. It begins dim, but grows in
intensity as the day goes on. It warms the hearts and lives
of those it touches, and we can always count on its presence. God, help us to value our friendships and teach us
how to nurture them so they will grow. Just as the sun
helps the flowers grow in the springtime, so too do we
need to be uplifted by those we call friends. We pray that
the halls of our school will be filled year after year with
the vibrant energy of friendships that blossom daily.

Michael Batista
Xavier High School, Middletown, CT

Mandy Schmieder
Saint Pius X Catholic High School, Atlanta, GA

3
The Big Picture

Recalling God's Presence

- Creator God, be present with us at this time.
- We acknowledge your presence, Creator of the universe.
- Let us remember that when we gather in God's name, God is in our midst.

Prayers

I am the angel of the alleys,
of hot grates,
of anxious needles shooting joy into anxious arms.
I am the redeemer of those
who live an alternative lifestyle,
who eat cold garbage,
who kill and kill and kill because they know nothing else.
My God of the back alley,
I saw you sleeping in a cardboard box marked "Fragile"
and with an ailing hand you begged me for a dime.
My God of the streets
I saw you selling yourself and your children.
My God of the sky
I saw you on your twentieth floor
peering down at the masses
cigar in hand

faint smile
spitting on the lowly.
My God, my God
millennium approaches.

Scott Herring
John Carroll High School, Birmingham, AL

God,
Why do some people see others through hateful eyes, see
only the color of skin, the texture of hair, or the sound of
accent instead of trying to see beyond that? Sometimes
I feel like I'm the only one who feels that prejudice is
wrong, not only against Blacks, Hispanics, or Jews, but
what about gays, Christians, Muslims, women, children,
Asians, and every other race, religion, or creed. God,
please help people realize that these prejudgments are
wrong. Let them learn to love, no matter what's on the
outside.

Grecia Mercedes
Saint Michael Academy, New York, NY

O God, I used to dream of simple things
That made life a joy to live.
When I was young, nature could be my playground;
And I never grew tired of being outside.
But as I got older, I grew greedy
And lost sight of what was important: You!
I got caught up with material things.
No more did simple things seem to satisfy.
O God, grant that I might be able to
Seek out the simple and only the complex that is good
      for me.
Help me, God, to seek out you and find what you
Intend me to be in life. Amen.

Jillian Baio
Mount Saint Dominic Academy, Caldwell, NJ

The wind stirs the hair on my head as it blows through
      the screen.
The light just breaking opens up the world to me;
      it lets me in.
The stars nestle back far in the sky and seem to fade away
      with the upcoming sun.
The world around me, God, is so vast and wonderful.
It is host to love and hate, peace and war, poverty and
      luxury.
The world is also full of people just like me—confused,
      awed, aware. Help us to wake up every morning
      to the wind and sunlight,
   and when you deem right, let us go on our way to the
      stars.
Amen.

Bridget Joyce
Saint Pius X Catholic High School, Atlanta, GA

Love is not for the lovely alone;
love is for those who need it;
those who have heard the Master's call,
yet, somehow, failed to heed it.

They are the envious, they are the cruel,
the vindictive, and the greedy;
they are the hungry, they are the poor,
they are God's most needy.

It's easy to love the lovely,
the sweet, the good, and the true;
but the ones who curse and hate you,
they need loving too.

Dannelle Melgar
Saint Joseph Notre Dame High School, Alameda, CA

Dear God,
Help us to see you in all people.
Help us to see you in the unborn, and to realize that life is
        precious at the very beginning.
Help us to see you in those with a different background,
    and to respect different races and their customs,
    realizing that we were all created by you in
        your likeness.
Help us to see you in our elders
    and to treat the gift of life with supreme reverence,
    and to see the gifts that older people have to offer.
Help us to see you in members of the other sex
    and to respect them as persons, not objects.
Help us to see you in the poor and homeless,
    and to aid them in whatever way possible.
Help us to see you in the outcasts
    and to reach out to those who are left out
        and unpopular.
Help us to see you in those who belong to
        different religions
    and to use our common interests for the
        common good.
God, help us not to judge or discriminate,
    but to greet people with open minds and hearts.
Help us to see others as you see them,
    without discrimination and with love.

Ben Hayes
Bishop Dwenger High School, Fort Wayne, IN

Dear God,
I would like to pray for peace and justice among the people of the world. I want racism to leave us, and for us to
understand that we are all brothers and sisters of the same
race, the human race. Hear this, God. Amen.

Micheal Milan
Bishop Loughlin Memorial High School, Brooklyn, NY

As I walk east,
Past the countryside
I feel the presence of God,
Sacred spirit to whom I confide.

As I walk east,
Past the steady rush of the stream,
I ask my God,
"Is this all a dream?"

God says, "Yes, it is.
Look at the water; doesn't it glisten?
What is wrong? Tell me; I'll listen."

I ask my God,
"Will the time ever come
When I can look to my neighbor,
And say we are one?"

God, teach the people now
Not to take, but to borrow
The gift of this world
That belongs to tomorrow.

God bestow in me the gift
That I can share with others
To let the people know
That they are all my sisters and brothers.

God, feed me your loving bread,
Give me drink in your chastening cup.
Suddenly a breeze blows by,
To present God's reply,
But then I wake up.

Allyson Reaves
Saint Vincent de Paul High School, Petersburg, VA

You've lived on earth how many years
enjoyed laughter . . . and tears.
Do you think it's fair taking fun away
from kids aborted each day?

You may not think—or know—but
just the same—even so . . .
you're killing kids not born
lives shattered, destroyed—torn.

Questioning how you'll support it?
Still no reason to abort it.
People are waiting to adopt,
take a second—step back—stop!

You got pregnant one day
not the kid's fault! It shouldn't pay!
Pregnant against your will? I understand,
but still . . .

Choose life—be one of the few
remember—that could have been you!

Jennifer Bierl
Saint Vincent's, Springbrook, NY

Kind God,
I thank you for all the blessings you have so richly given
me. So I come to you with a heavy heart this time. There's
a lack of justice in the world. People are more concerned
with padding their own pockets than with judging others
fairly. We see evidence of this in the legal system that gov-
erns us, and yes even in the church. God, I ask that you
guide us in the path that we should go. Show us that your
way is a better way, and if we follow it we will be much
better off. This I pray in the name of your Son, Jesus
Christ. Amen.

Mike Silmon
Aquinas High School, Southgate, MI

God,
Grant us your wisdom. We do not ask that you help us
through the day; rather, we ask you to give us the compassion to help others through difficult times. Teach us
understanding so we may see Christ in all people. Jesus
showed us forgiveness; help us to forgive and love our
enemies. We do not ask that you give us peace, but grant
us the ability to love all people so that we can find peace
ourselves. Teach us responsibility and help us to remember to care for your people and your earth. We ask this in
Christ's name. Amen.

Rebecca Braun
McNicholas High School, Cincinnati, OH

O Lord, help us to cherish each moment of our lives.
In the midst of suffering and pain,
give us strength and guidance.
With every action, let us find peace
within our souls
and comfort within our hearts.
Help us learn forgiveness,
and bless those who have wronged us.
Grant us mercy and compassion
toward our enemies,
and loving kindness for those for whom we care.
Let us enjoy the endeavors of life,
and live each day to the fullest,
for we have sacrificed a day of our lives,
which is forever gone,
in order to accomplish our dreams.
Amen.

Rani Thykkuttathil
Holy Names Academy, Seattle, WA

Hunger and pain haunt our world today.
Won't the starvation ever go away?
In a world where love and peace should make us one,
How did the world come so undone?
We try to rebuild a world we destroy,
But each time we try, we play at it like a toy.
People die because they don't have enough to eat,
And many are the ones we meet on the street.
We want the power to be in our own hand,
So we can't see the hunger and pain
In God's one and only vanquished land.

Sara Kubik
Marquette High School, Bellevue, IA

Realizing
that the perfect world God created
is not always so perfect

that the things we thought were meant to be
do not always work out

that our hopes and dreams for the future
do not always come true

and then finally realizing
that God created everything perfect
and created us to choose
and if we choose
to love and to hope and to dream
for things that may or may not ever happen

then we are living life
as it was truly meant
to be lived.

Robin Grady
Wahlert High School, Dubuque, IA

When I was younger I lived in the South. Two other girls my age lived on the same street. We were around six or seven years old and in first grade. Each of us loved playing hopscotch and jump rope. But that is where the similarities had to stop. At a very young age I was forced to deal with a very real problem: racism.

One of the girls was not allowed in or around the other's home. At six years old, I couldn't understand why. She loved to build sand castles in the street and play hide-and-go-seek in the woods as much as we did. I never really understood why each time I would walk into this one girl's house, the other would have to wait at the end of the driveway. The look on her face was one I could never recreate. Looking back on it, I guess I still feel like I'm that six-year-old girl. Because I still don't understand why the three of us could never play together.

But it taught me a great lesson about life. I learned at a very young age to care about people for who they are and what they are like on the inside, not by the color of their skin. Every time I find myself judging someone without knowing what's inside, I see so clearly in my head that girl and the look on her face.

Katie
Our Lady of Lourdes High School, Poughkeepsie, NY

Gracious God,
I ask of you to eliminate the evils of prejudices in every form. I ask that you open up the eyes of those who refuse to see you in everyone. I ask that you open up the ears of those who refuse to hear you in everyone. I ask that you open up the mouths of those who refuse to speak for you to everyone. Open up the hearts of those who refuse to love. Unite us again. Amen.

Michael L. Harmon
Bishop Noll Institute, Hammond, IN

Dear God,
You said that you created each of us different and that we are special. Then why do some people consider me different just because of my color, my race, my religion, or the clothes I wear? I remember that you also were an outcast and that you didn't try to hide it from anyone. You stood up for your beliefs and even died for them. Help me to stand up and not hide my beliefs either. I am still young and don't fully understand everything, but I trust that you know what is best for us. Amen.

David Le
Elder High School, Cincinnati, OH

Dear God,
We thank you for all that you have given us,
For the earth, the plants, and the animals,
And all your gifts that go unappreciated.

We thank you for the confidence you grace us with
By giving us care of your world.
However, we are not ready to lead without your help.
We still make too many mistakes,
And we need your guidance.

Help us see injustice with the eyes you gave us,
Help us listen to what matters,
Help our mouths not speak lies and deceive.

But most important,
Guide us to do more than see, listen, or speak,
Guide us to use our hands to do something positive for
    this world,
Guide us not to step aside from responsibility,
But rather to do our part
in making this a better place for all your children. Amen.

Eric Becker
Brother Rice High School, Bloomfield Hills, MI

Loving mother God,
I praise and respect you for your strength and courage.
Please help your daughters on earth.
Many are suffering, afraid, alone,
whether from abuse at home,
harassment at work,
jealousy among friends,
rape and murder in all areas of the world,
or even a simple broken heart.
Depression and despair often rule the lives of women.
Please grant your daughters the strength to say no
to the violence that happens to many every day.
Thank you, mother God!
Your peaceful grace helps us see our self-worth.
Please continue to guide us toward peace in your love.

Karen Petruska
Visitation Academy, Saint Louis, MO

God,
Thank you for the life I live. Please help me to live this life
with a positive outlook each day. Help me to develop into
the person I'd like to be: an honest, giving, and healthy
individual. To find this me, please grant me the courage
to stand up against society and peer pressure as I draw up
my own set of values. As I grow through my teenage
years, help me to form a special relationship with you
that I will be able to build on. Teach me to respect myself,
as well as others, and to treat them in a way I would like
to be treated. Most of all, help me to develop your gift of
love so that it may affect others in a special way—just like
the way your love for me has had a great impact in my
life.

Kaitlyn Pratt
Archbishop Williams High School, Braintree, MA

Jeff: "Hello."
Jesus: "How do you do?"
Jeff: "I'm a little confused."
Jesus: "About what?"
Jeff: "Well, tell me what heaven is like?"
Jesus: "It's beautif . . ."
Jeff: "No, no, no! Not what it looks like, but what it feels like. Is it like a soft gentle white cloud floating about, or is it like a bird soaring high above? Is it as beautiful as a springtime rainbow, or as sensuous as the melodious tones of Beethoven? Is it like a great awakening or a long silent sleep? Can I fly about, jump from petal to petal like a summer bee? Will I be alone in the dark, or will I be comforted by friends and family? Will all of the little wars inside of me be resolved? Can I ever go back, be an angel or a saint? What is outside our universe, what is the relationship between space and time? Before the Big Bang, what existed? Is time a function of life, or is it just a silly human idea? What about God? Is he a man, woman, thing, idea? If he is the Creator, who created him? Why doesn't God have an equal or someone greater? Why can't . . ."
Jesus: "Take it easy, everything will be shown to you."
Jeff: "When?"
Jesus: "When the time is right for you."

Jeff Senkevich
Cardinal Newman High School, Santa Rosa, CA

Thank you, God, for the beautiful gift of glass. It is one of the most perfect objects; it is a symbol of life. Sometimes it is clear, revealing everything. At other times, it is dull or dirty and hard to see through. It is capable of so many uses. Help me to realize the strength and fragility of life.

Tony Kullen
Fordham Preparatory School, Bronx, NY

What is it like to always see
Someone faster and smarter
On the other side?
All of us are different.
God sees our hidden talents
And knows what we can do,
Even if it happens a little slower
Or a little differently than we expected.
All of us are different.
God makes us this way.

But now without a little help,
I can't walk, so I ride in a chair.
He can't see and uses a cane.
She is slow, so she takes her time.
You can't always see the differences with the naked eye,
But all of us are different.
God makes us this way.
Thank you, God!

Michelle Gricus
Carmel High School, Mundelein, IL

God,
Help me to understand why:
there is war instead of peace,
there is hatred instead of love,
there is lying in place of the truth.
Give me the courage, strength, and wisdom
to teach others the meaning of peace, love, and truth,
so we can make this world a better place for all to live in
harmony. Amen.

Sean Johnson
Boston College High School, Dorchester, MA

62

Dear God,
In hopes that their lives will soon grow in blessings and good fortune, please bless the homeless and those less fortunate. May those who are poor in spirit and heart find their way to God and act in God's ways. For this, I pray. Amen.

Carlos Eason
Daniel Murphy High School, Los Angeles, CA

Red asphalt.
Blood stains the street from the night before,
And tonight they'll be back to even up the score.

An innocent kid was shot in the spine,
Even though he has to be in a wheelchair, the gangsters
    don't mind.

You can hear a baby crying while his mother smokes
    a joint,
He may grow up to do just the same, so what's the point?

The teen down the street tries to buy a gun,
He wants to settle an argument that he had
    with someone.

Some young people today are ignorant and dumb,
Because they think that killing someone is fun.

There's so much pressure today to belong,
We'll do anything to prove ourselves even though it's
    wrong.

Ryan Boehm
Saint Genevieve High School, Panorama City, CA

Creator,
Let us not forget
why we live.
Let us pray.
Let us not abandon
our brothers and sisters.
Let us love.
Let us not deny
our faith in you.
Let us believe.
Let us not beg
for the glories of the world.
Let us be humble.
Let us not sin
and persecute others.
Let us forgive.
Let us not die
for evil.
Let us live for Christ.

Anthony Piscitiello
Cotter High School, Winona, MN

There are reasons why thunder thunders, why lightening strikes, why snow snows, why earthquakes quake, why people die—we must accept these as some sort of miracle of Jesus. Jesus is special, and so is life. So if we live our life like Jesus, we too shall be special. Doubts about faith naturally happen when tragedies shred our faith. But that's what's so special about belief in Jesus and the way. Belief helps us know in our heart that what happens can lead to good. And we must try to understand as much as we can, and stay thirsty.

Jason Fragala
Bishop Ireton High School, Alexandria, VA

Bridges help join places together.
Bridges join cultures and customs of different people
    together.
Sometimes I wish that life was more full of bridges.
When people fight or argue,
I wish a bridge could bring them together.
I wish we could bridge the gap of hatred in the world
    today.
Through Jesus, Amen.

Nikki Brummett
Holy Rosary Academy, Louisville, KY

I call you. I'm a voice in nature, a silent whisper of faith. Sometimes you run from my open hands. I call you in service. I am present in the wind and warmth of the sun. I'm calling you to a life of peace. My voice is in the hills, the mountains, and lakes. It is in the face of a mother struggling to conquer hunger. It is the warmth of a father's hands, striving to keep his family warm in their little thatched hut. I call you within the deserts of Mexico and in the kindness of oppressed people.

    I call you from this material world to a world of true happiness, one that gratifies the soul and mind. My voice is calling you to be a servant for Christ, a messenger, a guide, and a life-lover. I'm calling you to reach out and be concerned for the world. Love all people, and never let go of my voice. It may start as a whisper but become a yell. Answer it. Come to me. Live out your true destiny. Become one with yourself, God, and society. Never reject my voice. You can learn so much about yourself and others from such a small whisper inside this troubled world.

Jonathan Huth
Saint John High School, Gulfport, MS

In the distance, I see peace
A place where people can be friends
Where tranquillity will always reign
And where life never ends.

A time of great wonder
Where life is allowed to shine
Where children's laughter echoes loudly
There's a reflection of mine.

A time of great love
People with love for each other
No more in conflict
Instead we're sister and brother.

In the distance I see peace
But only if I start with me
And with some help from up above
Only then can this peace come true.

Ashley Roman
Immaculata High School, Somerville, NJ

Blessed are those who do not shun their peers
or possess condescending attitudes toward them;
their joy is in helping, and their lives are meaningful.
They are like a pleasant fire
that glows happily and gives warmth to all in need.
But those who are cruel are a cold, dusty draft
adding only grief to a world
that desperately needs the flames of comfort.
Those who try reaching out will find joy
even in the smallest aspects of life,
but those who do not may remain clueless
to the meaning of life and to all the joys within it.

Charisa Smith
Villa Victoria Academy, Trenton, NJ

God of all that lives,
teach your people to care for the earth.
Teach them, and teach them well,
to respect their elders.
Guide each and every one of us
in your path of knowledge and wisdom.
Give us the courage
to face our most unwanted fears and the dangers in life.
Give us strength to overcome our weaknesses.
Help us not to take anything you have given us
    for granted.
Thank you, God, for loving us so much.
Thank you for giving us our life,
though at times we are undeserving.
Thank you for listening to my prayer
and to the prayers of each one of us.
May we all one day live with you in peace.
Amen.

Juliana Leon
Saint Catherine Indian School, Santa Fe, NM

Jesus died for all of us to live together: black, white, Spanish, Asian. Today we kill each other; we mock each other because of pure ignorance. We are dying slowly but surely, and death has no color! I pray for another tomorrow!

Dear God, my heart goes out to you, for you have never given up. So I pray for another tomorrow!

Young enough to be a child but old enough to pull a trigger—does that make any sense to you? *Love* is a strong word, but *hate* seems even stronger. Let us dwell on a great today while I pray for another tomorrow!

Natacha Agnant
Saint John's College High School, Washington, D.C.

When I feel like going to a party how come I have to get searched when I walk in? It's not like I own a weapon or anything of that nature. I don't try to portray myself as someone who is coming somewhere just to start trouble. I just want to have a good time. Why do things have to be that way?

When I walk into a store, why does the salesclerk continue to watch me out of the corner of his or her eye? Is it because he or she thinks I might need help, or is it standard store procedure, as it's called? If I need help, I know how to use my mouth to ask for help. If it is standard store procedure, how come the kid in the next aisle with the light complexion and the blonde hair isn't being followed like me? Why do things have to be that way?

When I walk down the street, how come the cops jump out of their cars to check if I have any weapons or drugs on me because I "fit the description of a known suspect in the area." Then after they find out that I don't carry a gun or sell drugs, they walk off like there is nothing wrong, no apology or anything. Why do things have to be that way?

Every time I feel that I or someone else has been treated wrong I ask God the question, Why do things have to be that way? Are the things people see on television the way they view us all? Why am I being treated wrongly for the acts of my brothers and sisters? Does the word *ignorance* mean anything? Ignorance is the reason I can't go anywhere without being searched. Ignorance is the reason I can't go into a store without being followed around. Ignorance is the reason the police look at me as just another drug dealer. Ignorance is the reason that things have to be that way.

Lazeric C. White
Saint Martin de Porres Academy, Chicago, IL

Even though times are hard
and we sometimes feel like no one is on our side,
we can make it.
Even though people we trusted
turn on us and we feel like the world is against us,
we can make it.
We can make it if we just believe.
We can make it if we just hold on.
We can achieve our goal.
We can tell God that we can make it.
We can make it, if we just believe!

Anonymous
West Philadelphia Catholic High School, Philadelphia, PA

God, help me to open my eyes widely, look about me, and see other people not blinded by color, not based on race. Help me to see each man as my brother, each person my equal, each woman my sister. Let me live my life with equality.

Jonna Kosalko
Bishop Noll Institute, Hammond, IN

Wake up, Black man!
Wake up, Black woman!
Learn of your greatness,
Your beauty,
Your true sense of self.
Know that you are the sons of Allah.
Know that you are the daughter of Yahweh,
Jesus is your brother,
The original man and woman,
The Adam and the Eve.
Wake Up.
Know Yourself.

Martin Luther King, Jr. cannot do it.
Malcolm X cannot do it.
Elijah Muhammad cannot do it.
No single messiah will save you.
You must become your own messiah.
Reach within to save yourself.
You have the power within you.
Make yourself victorious.
Make yourself triumphant.
Search within your soul,
The soul of God's own self.
The breath God breathed into your nostrils,
The breath of life,
Know that you were made in God's image,
The very image of God.
You are God and human.
You then become extensions of God.
The power of God is the power in you.
Rise, Black people, Rise!
Wake up!
This time the nation will hear.

Jasantonio Hindman
Saint Martin de Porres Academy, Chicago, IL

Dear God,
Please help our world leaders in their quest for peace. Give them strength and courage to complete their goal. Give us stamina to carry out God's will with peace and love in our hearts. Help us to start working toward this goal in our own lives—with our friends, peers, families, and in our own neighborhoods and schools. Today's world is often a hostile and degrading place, and your message is often countercultural. We see countries at war, gang wars, violence, and drugs, which all stand as obstacles to your vision of world peace. Help us to take the little, daily steps necessary to achieving world peace.

Mike Smith
Xavier High School, Middletown, CT

When I knew you, you were so full of life.
When I see you now, I see how life has taken its toll.

When I knew you, you had hopes and dreams.
When I see you now, I see that those dreams have faded
  into memories.

When I knew you, you were the friend who made
  me laugh.
Your smile was like the sun on a cold winter day.
When I see you now, tears have replaced that smile.

When I knew you, you touched my heart in a way no one
  else ever could.
When I see now I realize it is my turn to touch yours.

Shallan Cook
Saint Peter Chanel High School, Bedford, OH

Dear God,
While eating an orange the other day, I started to think
about different things. First, I was amazed by your idea for
the orange. It's beautiful, delicious, and so interesting.
Each slice contains hundreds of little bags of juice that
look like they were made and packed by hand. I thought
about how lucky I was to be able to eat, especially when
there are people starving in this world. I realized also that
I need to appreciate all the good things you have put in
my life. Thanks for helping me find you through that
orange.

Freddy Viera
Fordham Preparatory School, Bronx, NY

Dear God,
In a world filled with so much noise and confusion,
please give me the strength to make myself be heard. So
often people shy away from saying what they feel, or
standing up for what they believe in; they hide in the
shadows, relying on others to be their voice. So many
times that person in the shadows has been me. God, I
need your guidance to help me achieve the power to step
out from the shadows into the action of the world, to let
my feelings be known, to stand up for what is right, and
to be a voice to be heard.

Anne-Marie Bowen
Saint Pius X Catholic High School, Atlanta, GA

Natalie Leoni
Boylan Catholic High School, Rockford, IL

4

Addressing God

Recalling God's Presence

- The God who empowers dwells within us.
- Let us remember that the God of the universe lives among us.
- A kind and merciful God is in our midst as we pray.

Prayers

Dear God,
As the sweet breath of dawn escapes across the land and the first rays of the sun's light kiss the earth, help me to appreciate the beauty of this budding morning. Help me to see the glorious beauty that exists in everyone and everything.

This is your creation, and it is deserving of my love. There is a singular peace and beauty about each day, a singular magnificence with the rise of the sun each morning. Every sun is a new sun, and all the light streaming from it, shedding its warmth is new light on a new day.

With each new day, new sun, new light, there is also a new me. I grow and change with the passing of the sun.

And in its new light each day I am baptized again in the beauty and love of God and God's earth.

Kevin Mullally
Saint Pius X Catholic High School, Atlanta, GA

Is that you, God?
Are you really here, with me?
Are you in my joy and laughter,
And the sparkle in my eye?

Is that you, God?
Are you in my hurt and
sorrow, and the tears
that slip from my eye?

Sometimes, I don't know,
I'm supposed to believe, but
deep down, do I truly believe?
I want to.

God, are you everywhere?
Is it you that makes the sun
reflect on the rippling waves?
Are you here?

Do you change the colors of
leaves in the midst of the
autumn wind?
Tell me, is it you?

Doubt is not the feeling here.
It's awe and wonderment.
I'm totally mystified.
Are you in everything?

You *are* here, God; it *is* you!

Jill Bowers
Sacred Heart Academy High School, Mount Pleasant, MI

Dear God,
I don't know how to tell you how I feel. You know everything anyway. I hope you know I love you even if I don't
live like your Son. It's hard sometimes to decide between
you and my friends. It's really hard to put you into my life
without feeling like a religious fanatic. I know you love
me and, God, I really love you, too. Please don't be upset
if I don't look your way. It's hard for me.

I just want to say thanks, I guess. You've always been
there for me, and I feel safe knowing that. And I know
you're always trying to let me find my own way to you. I
really don't see how you put up with me at times. I just
want to let you know that when I do things you don't
like, it's not to go against your word or anything; it's usu-
ally because I get confused. It's my way of asking for help.
I'm glad you give it to me.

Don't worry, I'll find my way to you. I have to. I
know I couldn't live without your love and strength to
guide me.

Colleen McMonagle
Saint Rose High School, Belmar, NJ

Dear God,
I don't know who my friends are.
I don't know who to trust.
I've been betrayed by so many.
Yet, you want me to forgive.
If you love me, why would you want to hurt me?
Do believe me when I say I want to believe in you.
But how can I believe in something that I don't even
     know is there?
Will you help me to understand
and help me to believe in you?

Megan O'Malley
Saint Teresa's Academy, Kansas City, MO

Dear God,
Please guide me always
in the path of your love.
To walk in the light
and shrug from the darkness.

Help me to never be blind
to real beauty:
the beauty in every raindrop,
in every soul, in every person.

Teach me
to look past the shiny wrappers
and discover
the treasure inside all of us.

Thank you, God,
for sharing your breath of life with me.
Strengthen me
to share this breath with others.
Amen.

MaryAnn Taurino
Stella Maris High School, Rockaway Park, NY

O Great Spirit, guide me on my paths,
Let my heart flower like a meadow of wisdom,
Fill my soul with the breath of your greatness,
Quench my thirst with the rain of love,
Make my body dance to the rhythm of earth's heartbeat,
And give me the strength of northern winds,
So as I journey through my life,
I may always praise you,
And live in a peaceful harmony with your creation.
Amen.

Magda Polkowska
Immaculate Conception High School, Lodi, NJ

God, when I talk to you
I feel like a book;
Me, reading my problems to you,
You, turning the pages.

God, I trust you with everything,
Knowing you will always
Watch over my shoulder
As the day's obstacles overcome me.

God, I depend on you in tough times
Because you will help me through.
The days seem to pass by more easily
With a true friend like you.
Amen.

Debbie Granaghan
Saint Mary's Regional High School, South Amboy, NJ

I believe in the God of heaven
and in the God inside all of us.
I believe in Jesus Christ,
the savior and the light of our life,
who came to us in this world
to guide us to the Reign of God.
I believe in the miracle of life
and of the everyday things we see here on earth.
I believe in the guidance of God
as I ride this roller coaster called life.
I believe in the goodness of people,
even those who do not show goodness in their heart,
for they too are children of God.
I believe through the grace of God
I will succeed in my life
and in this uncertain world.

Irish E. Trinidad
Ramona Convent Secondary School, Alhambra, CA

From the heavens above,
to the earth below,
God surrounds us.
When times are bad,
and things go wrong,
God is with us.
God is there when we sleep,
and every moment of our life.
God is a friend,
someone we can turn to.
God is always there to talk to.
All we have to do is have faith
and believe in ourself.

Michael Fauteux
Xavierian Brothers High School, Westwood, MA

Dear God,
Everyday I see things . . .
great and wonderful beings . . .

From the giant trees that stand tall and strong . . .
to the little flowers upon the lawn . . .

From the oceans so grand . . .
to the seas and the land . . .

All things great and small . . .
you are the one who made them all . . .

When I see the creatures of the land . . .
in awe I often stand . . .

The sea's waters are so blue . . .
to a baby that is born anew . . .

You bring them together in a cosmic stew . . .
everything I see I owe to you . . .

Mike Look
Bishop Moore High School, Orlando, FL

Love squared = gold
Love + one = family
Love - one = mourning
Love halved = heartache
Love divided by one = commitment
Love divided by many = friendship
Love times zero = loneliness
Love times two = faithfulness
Love times infinity = God

F. J.
Mercy High School, Riverhead, NY

Be happy for your legs—for you can walk;
there are those who only wish they could.
Be happy for you have parents;
there are some who only wish they could be loved.
Be happy for you can see;
there are some who don't know what the world looks like.
Be happy for you know Christ;
there are those who are lost and can't find him.
Be happy for you have life;
there are those that don't get the chance.

Yvonne Casanova
Providence High School, San Antonio, TX

God,
You plant us in your garden of goodness and carefully
place us on earth. You nourish us with your goodness and
shine your rays of truth upon us. We are all made beautiful in your light. If we grow along the right path, God, we
will forever bloom in your glory!

Liz Rogers
O'Connell School, Galveston, TX

Dear God,
The first thing I hear when I wake up is an alarm;
In that sharp sound I hear your voice.

As I go downstairs and walk into the kitchen,
I hear my father preparing breakfast for me;
In my father's action I hear your voice.

As I run to the corner to catch the bus,
I hear the call of two small birds;
In their cries I hear your voice.

As I walk into the hallway in school,
I am kindly greeted by my friends;
In their acceptance I hear your voice.

Two times throughout the day,
I hear the sound of the school bell;
In its ring I hear your voice.

At night, during dinner,
My parents inquire about how my day went;
In their love and concern I hear your voice.

I am thankful to hear your call
and to appreciate your splendor.
Help me to always answer your call
through my love for you, my friends, and my family.
Amen.

Alaine Gherardi
Academy of the Holy Angels, Demarest, NJ

December 13th
Crystal spread so evenly
Upon the glossy streets.
This is where the love of God
And kindness of humankind meet.

The tips of autumn's fingers
Brush the greening trees.
They burn so bright,
Through fog and light,
They set my mind at ease.

The water pulls lovingly at my ankles
Wanting me to feel what it feels.
And at God's name gently spoken
Every proud mountain kneels.

Because God's name is love;
Love that paints the sky
Across the dimming horizon
Just like a sleepy lion's eye.

Love is what has brought me here;
And shown my heart the way
Of solitude and gratitude
For the blessings of the day.

How can we miss a star-filled sky?
Or a sunset painted gold?
How can we not love the birth of new?
Or witness the death of old?

The mountain is tall and sturdy,
The blade of grass so small.
They are both of no such power
As the God that made them all.

How God loves us so perfectly!
Gave us beauty on earth!
Wants our hearts to feel at ease,
Wants our minds to know our soul's good worth.

Rachel Mosman
Mount Saint Mary High School, Oklahoma City, OK

Believe what you believe
Live how you live
Feel as you feel
Enter.
One who really knows
experiences
the pain of mixed emotions
vibrant opinions
lingering sensations
for the living God.
People who have been on
this journey can freely love themselves
and others in harmony,
together, as one.
Amen

JoAnn Lavenz
Wahlert High School, Dubuque, IA

I believe in one God,
Both father and mother,
Who synchronized the events of Creation.
I believe in the Son
And in the Spirit who fills us with love.
I believe that all three beings are one.
I believe Jesus Christ was born and that he died for us;
Living his life in the full holiness of God,
And by his death opening the gates of heaven.
I believe that Jesus rose again
And that one day all will be judges in the fairness of God.
I believe in the forgiveness of sins
And in the existence of heaven.

Sarah Korkowski
Holy Names Academy, Seattle, WA

My God, my God, where are you?
In my darkest hours, I cried for you, but you didn't
    answer.
Do my petitions fall on deaf ears?
Do you choose to ignore me?
What have I done to anger you, my God?
I believe in you.
From the bottom of my heart, I call for you.
Yet you do not answer.
Where are you, my God?
Send me a sign—
a bird singing in the sun, a smile from a stranger;
tell me you're here.
O God, answer me.
I've done all that I can.
In faith, I leave the rest in your divine providence.

Ma. Katrina M. Dy
Saint Dominic Academy, Jersey City, NJ

Holy One,
The Chosen One
Our light in darkness,
Our peace in time of pain,
Our love in times of hate,
Savior, Christ,
The coolness of a summer's breeze,
The calm beneath a storm,
Mother, Father, Sister, Brother,
Understanding, all loving,
A person of hope,
And the creator of youth,
Lord, Holy Spirit, Teacher
Friend

Stephanie De Leon
Academy of the Sacred Heart, Bloomfield Hills, MI

God,
We don't realize the effect that people have upon us in our everyday lives. We seem to forget to look back on the glories of God's love. So grant me, God, this prayer in hopes that it will remind me at times how lucky I am.

In the morning I get ready for school. I roll out of bed and put on my clothes, not realizing that some people don't even have a bed to get out of or clothes to change into; it's just a normal day to me.

Upon entering my house, I head straight for the refrigerator, not realizing that I pass the same old guy everyday who waits for the city bus, or that people are starving in our world; it's just a normal day to me.

In the evening, I do my homework in hopes of getting good grades, and I eat dinner with my family, not realizing that some people don't have money for education or loved ones to sit at a table with; it's just a normal day to me.

Then I go to bed, and I thank you, God, for this day. After all, it's just another normal day for me. Amen.

Karen Scheller
Mater Dei High School, Evansville, IN

There is a voice, deep in my heart.
It leads me and guides me all of my life.
There is a voice, inside of my soul.
It is calm and kind, never getting too loud.
There is a voice, within my spirit.
Telling me all the secrets of my heart.
There is a voice, I trust it with my life.
There is a voice. It is yours, God.
Amen.

Erin Gardner
Saint Mary's Regional High School, South Amboy, NJ

A life without faith
Is a candle without a flame.
God gives everyone a candle.
It is up to us to light them
And use them to light the way.

Some of us never light our candle.
We walk in fear of the darkness.
Not even our shadows seem to appear.

Yet the one who lights the candle
Is followed by God, and led down
The right pathway.

Nicole Curtiss
Marian High School, Bloomfield Hills, MI

I watched a man die today
for reasons I do not know.
And even though I didn't know his name,
I shuddered from head to toe.

I watched a man die today.
He blinded me with his light.
And even though I didn't know his name,
tears made me lose my sight.

I watched a man die today,
with nails driven in his palm.
And even though I didn't know his name,
he looked so peacefully calm.

I watched a man die today,
with a crown of thorns on his head.
And even though I didn't know his name,
I knew that he would rise from the dead.

Jason Re
Bishop Ireton High School, Alexandria, VA

Shh, be quiet.
Sit still, and you can hear God.
Look closely,
concentrate, and you can see.
You're trying too hard.
Open your mind,
let your eyes wander,
focus on the world around you.
Let the sounds pour freely into your ears.
Do you hear the song of that bird?
That is God singing.
Do you see the children laughing?
That is God laughing.
Do you smell the spring flowers?
That is God beckoning.
God is everywhere.
When you are in despair,
God is with you.
Look outside your window, and God will appear.
Not as an apparition,
a demon,
or a light,
but in the song of the children skipping rope,
and those playing ball in the park,
the homeless man begging for change down on
        the corner,
and the person with AIDS struggling in the face of death.
Abstract yet present,
God is not hard to see,
a light full of color,
magnificent hues.
from black to white,
God sees no boundaries.
God is in everything
Everything is in God.

Michael Elmer Bulleri
Sacred Heart Cathedral Preparatory, San Francisco, CA

Dear Jesus,
Sometimes I think about all that I have been through,
And I wonder if things will ever be the same again.
I think of the joys and sadness I have experienced;
But what I will never forget is the strength
You have given me through those times
And the feelings of security
That come from knowing you are always by my side.
From a loving and grateful heart, thank you!

Jessica Nguyen
Little Flower Catholic High School for Girls, Philadelphia, PA

Dear God,
Thank you for the sun.
Thank you for the Son.
Both are vital to life.
Without each, we could not exist.
The sun gives us the light.
The Son is the light.
From the light plants grow.
From the Light grow the plants of your Kingdom.
We devour the plants and other creatures that devour
    the plants.
We devour the fruits of his knowledge for they are
    eternal food.
The sun is our life.
The Son is our life.
Thank you, gracious God.

Robert Traxler
Christian Brothers High School, Memphis, TN

If you've ever looked at someone
and saw that the goodness is inside,
no matter what was on the outside,
then you've seen God . . . with your eyes.

If you've ever heard a song,
that brings joy and hope to everyone around you,
no matter who says it's too stupid or holy,
then you've heard God . . . with your ears.

If you've ever eaten your relatives' cooking,
and found the care and love baked into everything,
no matter how awful it tastes,
then you've tasted God . . . with your mouth.

If you've ever smelled lilacs and roses,
growing in a grassy, green meadow, and you jumped
    and played
no matter how silly you looked,
then you've smelled God . . . with your nose.

If you've ever recognized that Jesus is in everyone,
and you've done that extra good thing
and gone that extra mile, no matter how hard the road,
then you've felt God . . . with your heart.

Laura A. Laskowski
Queen of Peace High School, Burbank, IL

God, you have been with me since before dawn. You created me in your image, a precious mystery, one of endless, yet timeless moments, one of many miracles granted.

God, you have been with me since sunrise, shaping my mind, leading me down a path to follow, yet never saying a word, quietly setting a foundation of morals, values, and lessons in friendship and leadership.

God, you have been with me when the sun set, when
things were peaceful and harmonious, when you may
have been left in the shadows of my happiness, not forgotten, yet ever-present in my joy.

God, you have been with me when the sun went
down, when there was no light to see, when I was at my
most pitiful, sorry, and unlovable state, when I knew
nothing would change, and I would remain alone. You
came out of the shadows and picked the sun back up. You
took away my sadness, replaced it with a new beginning,
a new foundation of strength, wisdom, understanding,
and loyalty.

God, you have seen me at my best. You have seen my
worst. You have loved me through my rights and my
wrongs, forgiving and understanding me when I thought
it impossible. Help me to follow your examples and grant
me your mercy.

Laura Smith
Saint Bernard's High School, Saint Paul, MN

For all the times
you
sent
a perfect light
a perfect note
a perfect word
a perfect look
thank you.
Your simple gifts
make me
happy.

Anonymous
Academy of the Holy Names, Tampa, FL

Black of night
Unbroken.
Clouds
Covering the sky.
Sightlessness,
Darkness,
Fear.
Yet I know,
Soon,
The birds
Will again
Begin to sing
The music you wrote for them
And the sky
Light up like footlights
For their harmonious choir
And I will wake to the sun,
Shining above
In your heaven.
This I know
For all this is yours
Created by you
Especially for us
Every day.

Anne Needham
Academy of the Holy Cross, Kensington, MD

God,
At the times I am so angry at life,
I turn to you.
Sometimes, when life is so good,
I take your love and guidance for granted.
Oh, if only I could see you stand before me.

God,
When a loved one dies,
I turn to you,
but when all are healthy
and the thought of death doesn't cross my mind,
I sometimes take you for granted.
Oh, if only I could feel you touching my skin.

God,
When simple pains build up inside me,
I turn to you,
but when I wake up with no worries,
I sometimes take you for granted.
Oh, if only I could hear you whisper in my ear.

God,
Help me to see you with my heart.
Help me to feel you in my soul.
Help me to hear you in my breath.
So I won't have time to take you for granted.

Amy Lash
Seton Catholic High School, Chandler, AZ

Each day that goes by, something new arises. Most people strive to change themselves and others, always looking to change what they have for something better, never remembering exactly what they needed to change. We seldom stop and look back on what we have. Each morning I awake, the world is changing, but essentially remains the same. The sky is still blue, the clouds fill in all around. The sun rises and then sets just in time to make room for the moon and stars. The tides go in and out. I awake and am able to breathe and walk. None of this has changed. Each day I notice all these unchanging things around me. I see you, God, in these things and give thanks for them. Your love may change forms, but remains the same. Amen.

Tim Wozny
Bishop Noll Institute, Hammond, IN

I can see God.
Some people may criticize this,
and say it's not real,
but I can see God.
Others may say this is impossible,
but I see God in a different way.
God lives in us and all we are.
When I look at the sky,
I see divine splendor.
When I view creation,
I see sacred imagination.
When I look at the land,
I see God's love.
If seeing God in this way is not real,
then nothing is.

Stephen Valdes
Canevin Catholic High School, Pittsburgh, PA

Draw me a river
That flows over cool earth
And teases and taunts pebbles and stones
That deems chaos in the cold
And serenity in its warmth and glory.

Paint me a sky
In the setting of the sun
With brilliant colors fading
Into an endless dark cloak
Sprinkled with moon drops
That twinkle and bow
To the great guardian of the night.

Color me an ocean
Tranquil green
With foam-capped waves
Surrendering to the mighty sand
With a crashing defeat.

Bear me your soul
That holds all emotion
To pour into my eyes
And I will see
The river
The sky
The ocean
You will show me the world.

Rosie Mollica
Bishop Kearney High School, Brentwood, NY

Perhaps I have failed you;
Yet you have never failed me.
Perhaps I have betrayed you.
You can never betray me.
Perhaps I have forgotten you.
You always remember me.
I am a sinner,
But you are always here,
Always leading me,
Shining brightly,
Leading me to righteousness,
Encompassing me in your strength,
Reluctant to let me go,
Striving to change me,
Protecting me from danger,
Giving me hope,
Inviting me to live.
Your love, my God, is my strength.

Elvira Picrardo
Saint Agnes Academic School, College Point, NY

94

God is present throughout the land;
holiness and goodness are in all of creation.
God is visible in those who work for the well-being
    of others:
the compassionate, generous, and unselfish.
God is present in those who persecute others:
the ones most in need of God's guidance.
God is visible in all the children of the world:
the playful, growing, loving, and trusting.
God is present in those who are imperfect.
The loving arms of God continue to hold those who turn
    away.
Be thankful for the forgiveness of God!
Though people choose sin over love, they will not be
    abandoned.
Rejoice!
Humanity will never be without the love of our God!
We are the children of God for all eternity.

Grace Telcs
Holy Names Academy, Seattle, WA

God is eternal as the limits of the universe.
Through the darkness outstretched in the world today,
God's love shines through the cracks forever.
Like a supernova shining brightly for a short time,
we can feel God's love in great magnitude.
But when this star burns out,
we can look up to the sky
and see another star shining bright in the sky.
Praise be God for divine eternal love!

Ryan Dee
John F. Kennedy Catholic High School, Manchester, MO

This morning while stopped at a red light I impatiently flipped through the radio stations for a song I liked. My thoughts about the day were cluttered with anticipation and worries. When unable to find what I was listening for, in a huff, I clicked off the radio. As I sat there I realized that silence would be a beautiful song. There were no words to sing, no notes to hum, and no squabbles to distract me. In a moment, I found myself at ease in your presence. Dear God, help me to accept listening when I cannot hear, asking when I cannot know, looking when I cannot see. Make me aware of your presence, and help me turn to you in times of confusion. Amen.

Maria Wickenheiser
Lancaster Catholic High School, Lancaster, PA

Dear God,
I wonder on this rainy day
if anything I hold is true?
I can hear what is spoken,
feel what I touch,
learn what is taught,
need what I want,
get what I got,
see what is shown,
and love what is not.
So as I sit here and
watch the raindrops
weave their weary paths
and die.
I realize the only real
truth I hold is you.
Amen.

Jennifer Black
Cardinal Gibbons High School, Raleigh, NC

Dear God,
You are a forgiving God.
You must be to forgive me,
for I often wear you like a favorite shirt.
I keep you clean, neat.
I show you off to all my friends.
but then I grow tired of you.
And needing something new,
I put you away in my closet
on a hanger with which you are familiar,
and I dress myself in new attire,
a different costume for a different day,
until I suddenly rediscover you
(like I have so many times before).
Placing you lovingly upon my frame,
vowing to never remove you,
the cycle beings once again.

Joy Donnell
Mount de Sales Academy, Macon, GA

Dear God,
Sometimes it seems that my hopes and dreams
    will never be,
and then I hear a little voice inside me,
"Carry on."
I've been down this road so long
I always feels someone is telling me,
"Carry on."
Who is this voice that is telling me what to do?
That little voice can only be you.

Dina Episcopia
Fontbonne Hall Academy, Brooklyn, NY

God,
When I am searching for a reason to believe, lead me on
the way of belief. Help me not to doubt you or your ways.
When I am reluctant to practice my faith, give me encouragement in this time of doubtfulness. When I am angry
and confused about why I tend to believe rather than not
to believe, help me to feel comfortable making my beliefs
my own and to respect other's beliefs also.

Sarah Koves
Hill-Murray High School, Saint Paul, MN

I sit here today thinking
of all the things that could have been,
should have been,
would have been,
if I had just believed.
Your love for me was shining through,
and I was unable to see it.
Your strength in me was very strong,
but I failed to feel it.
Your voice within me showed me the way,
yet I could not hear it.
But that was then, and this is now,
and I have seen your love,
felt your strength,
and listened to your words.
I have truly seen the light in my family, my friends,
and especially you, my God.
Without your providence I would have never seen
the light of the world
that unites us all as one.

Janine Lavin
The Mary Louis Academy, Jamaica Estates, NY

Dear God, we pray to you for peace and love.
We strive for your encouragement and strength
    as we grow.
We ask for forgiveness of our sins,
and let us start a new beginning for your love.
We believe in Jesus as our role model.
Help us act and treat others as Jesus has shown.
We ask that our lives be filled
with happiness and joy for all our years to come.
And we pray that your faith and ours grow together.
Amen.

Dan Joyal
Xavierian Brothers High School, Westwood, MA

God,
Knowing you are here for me means so much.
You are the only one I know will never leave me.

When I feel lonely—
    I have you.

When my friends have left me—
    I have you.

When the world is against me—
    I have you.

When I feel no one loves me—
    I have you.

When I feel wonderful—
    I have you, too.

Let me not only know that you are with me, let me feel
your presence. Allow me to feel your nurturing arms comforting me forever and ever. Amen.

Alyssa Vona
Saint Mary's Regional High School, South Amboy, NJ

As a child I dreamed of reaching up and pulling a star right out of the sky. Stars represent hope. They are the light in the dark, and they remind me never to give up hope. Their light represents joy and happiness; the dark sky surrounding them represents pain and suffering.

There are many stars in the sky. Many of them are hard to see. This makes me realize there are many people in the world who are in need. These people cannot see the light, only the dark sky. I must reach out to them and help them find the light in the dark and make them happy.

I will always reach up for the stars. In the stars, I see God who is the light, the happiness, the joy, the hope. The stars are always present; so is God. If we cannot see the stars, then we need to look a little harder, a little farther, and a little deeper.

Marilee Kieda
Mercy High School, Farmington Hills, MI

Index

Dreams Alive
Prayers by Teenagers
Edited by Carl Koch

Over one hundred prayers and reflections by teenagers from all over the United States have been collected in *Dreams Alive*. These prayers could be used to start a class, focus prayer during a retreat or day of recollection, trigger a discussion, or inform parents and educators about the rich spirituality of teenagers.

ISBN 0-88489-262-X
6 x 9, 87 pages, paper, $4.95